Contents

What are your senses?

People and animals have senses to help them find out about the world. You use your senses to feel, see, hear, taste and smell. Your senses can warn you of danger.

Your senses are very important to you and other animals every day. This book is about the sense of sight. You are going to find out how it works and what you use it for.

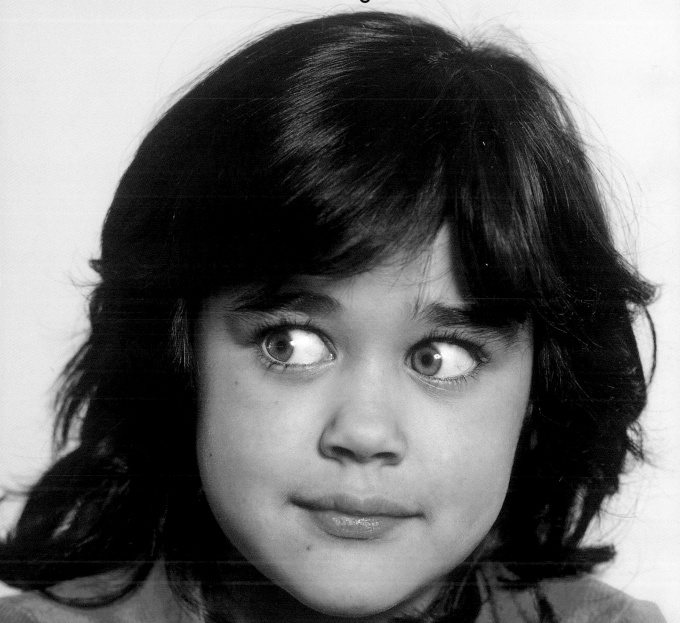

What do you use to see?

People use their eyes to see. You have two eyes at the front of your head. Animals also use their eyes to see. Animals' eyes are not always at the front of their head.

You use both of your eyes together so that you can see things near to you and things which are far away. Your **eyelashes** and **eyelids** keep your eyes clean.

How do you see?

Your eye is shaped like a ball. Most of the **eyeball** is inside your head. The eyeballs can move about so that you can see things at the side as well as in front of you.

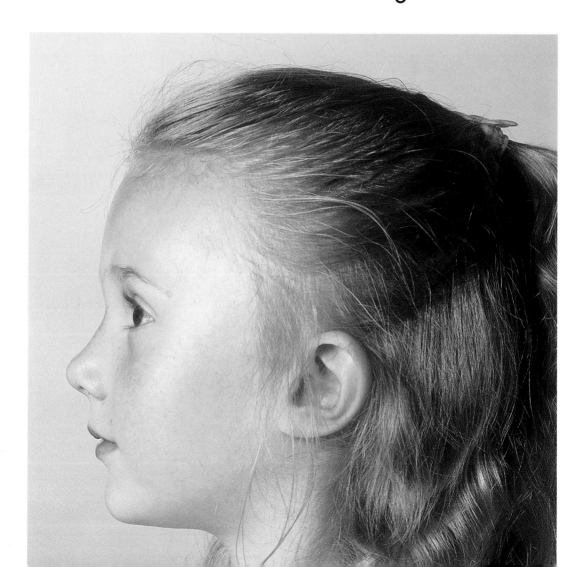

You need light to see. In the daytime you can see colours and shapes very well. At night you cannot see very well and things look grey or black.

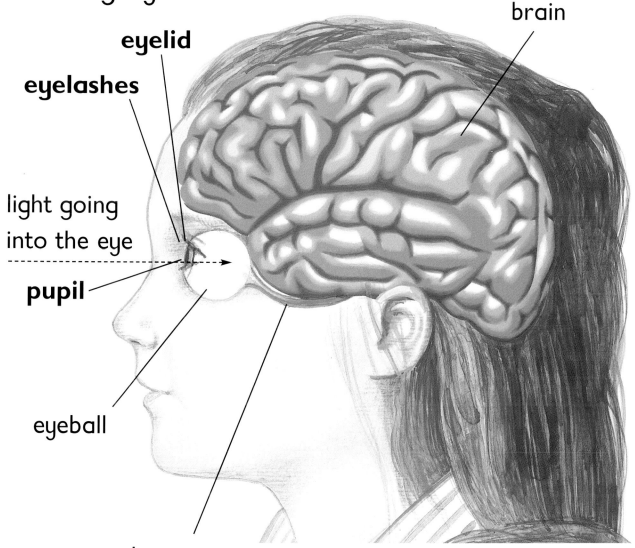

brain

eyelid

eyelashes

light going into the eye

pupil

eyeball

nerve takes messages
from the eye to the brain

Keeping safe

You use your eyes to warn you of danger. You can see cars on the road and smoke from fires. You can read warning signs which help you to stay away from danger.

People use their eyes to look for dangerous animals. Also you can often see if food is bad. Then you know that you must not eat it.

Do your eyes help you?

You use your eyes to read stories and to watch television. Your eyes help you to see balls when you are catching and kicking. You use your eyes if you work on a computer.

You need your eyes to use tools safely. They help you when you are cutting out and when you are measuring. Adults use their eyes when they are driving.

What can happen to your eyes?

Sometimes eyes do not work very well. When this happens people go to an **optician**. The optician makes glasses so that people can see properly.

Some people cannot see. They use their sense of touch and hearing to know where they are going. They use their fingers to feel a special kind of writing called **braille**.

How do animals see?

Your eyes are round like a ball. Birds' eyes are shaped like a long egg. This shape helps them to see far-away things very clearly.

Owls can turn their heads right round so that they can see all around. Flies have hundreds of parts to their very big eyes. They can see all around them.

Can animals see colours?

Some animals cannot see colours. Bulls cannot see colours, neither can cats, owls and bats. Cats have a little mirror in their eyes which helps them to see better at night.

Moles live underground where it is dark. They cannot see very well and they do not use their eyes very much. To make up for this they can hear sounds very well.

How do animals use their eyes?

Owls hunt at night and so they have special eyes which help them to see better in the dark. All animals use their eyes to watch for enemies.

Monkeys are like humans and have two eyes at the front of their head. This helps them to **focus** on the branches of trees as they swing up and down.

How do animals stay safe?

Animals that hunt usually have two eyes at the front of their head. Animals that are eaten by other animals often have eyes at the side of their heads.

Rabbits have eyes at the side of their heads so that they can see almost all around them. The **chameleon** can move each eye separately to look out for danger.

Investigating sight

Sit in a sunny place and look into a mirror. You will see that the **pupil** in your eye is very small. Try this in a darker place. You will see that the pupil is bigger. The eye is trying to let in more light.

This girl is using a **periscope** to see what is over her head. The picture in the top mirror shines onto the bottom mirror. What do you think she can see?

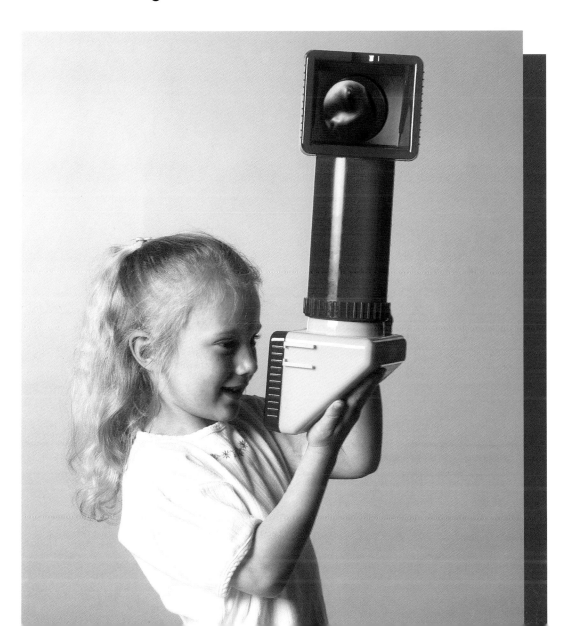

Playing tricks on your eyes

If animals are the same colour as things around them then they are difficult to see. We say that they are **camouflaged**. Look at the picture. Can you see the animal?

1 Draw round the bottom of a jar.

2 Cut out some circles.

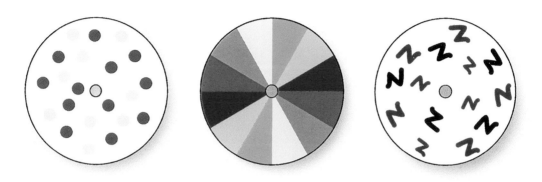

3 Put coloured patterns on your circles.

4 Push a pencil through
   the middle of the circles.

5 Spin your circles quickly. What do you notice?

Are you surprised by what you see? When you spin the wheels, different colours in the light bounce off into your eyes. Because the wheels go fast these colours join up.

Did you know?

Did you know that worms can tell the difference between light and dark and that snakes can see through their **eyelids**?

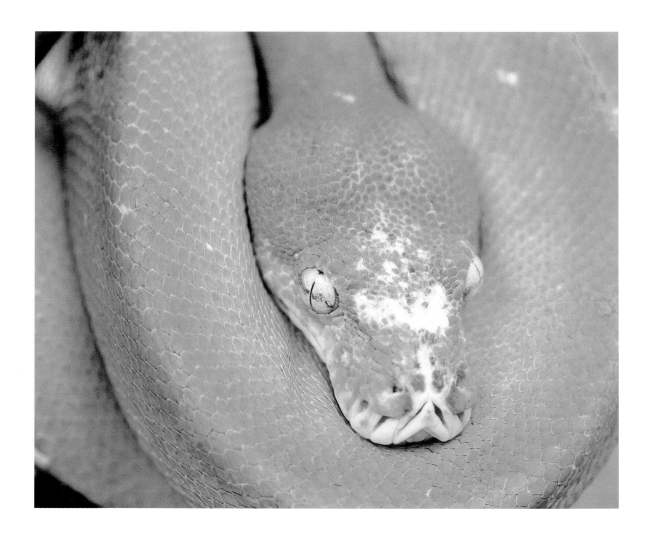

Did you know that flies can see hundreds of tiny pictures with their eyes?

Did you know that flatfish have eyes on top of their bodies?

Did you know that snails have eyes at the end of their long **feelers**?

Glossary

braille   a kind of writing with little bumps on the paper that blind people read with their fingers

camouflaged   something is camouflaged if you cannot see it very well because it is the same colour as the plants and land around it

chameleon   an animal which looks like a lizard and can change its colour

eyeball   the eyeball is round like a ball and about the size of a small plum

eyelashes   hairs on the end of your eyelids which keep dust and dirt out of your eyes

eyelids   pieces of skin which cover your eyes when you blink or when you are asleep

feelers   thin growths from the head of an insect which help the insect to know what is around it

focus   to be able to see something clearly

iris   the coloured part of your eye

nerve   something that carries messages from the body to the brain

optician   a person who can tell why your eyes are not working very well

pupil   the hole in the middle of the coloured part of your eye

periscope   a long tube or box with mirrors at the top and bottom. People use periscopes to see things which are over their heads.

Sense map

Light shines on the teddy and then goes through the little black hole called the **pupil**.

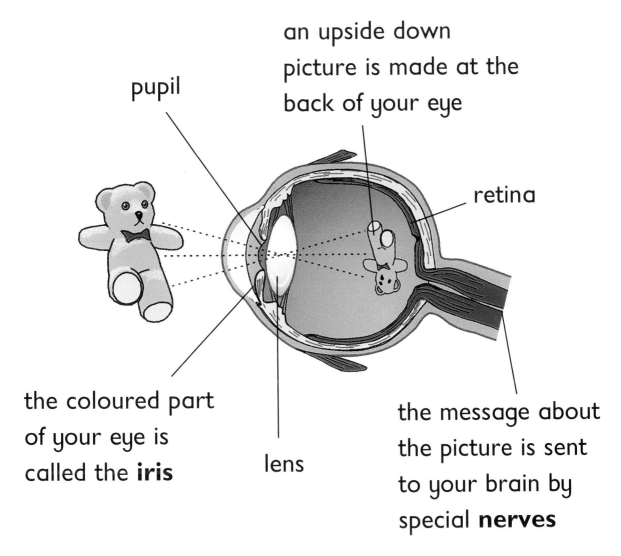

pupil

an upside down picture is made at the back of your eye

retina

the coloured part of your eye is called the **iris**

lens

the message about the picture is sent to your brain by special **nerves**

Index